ZONG GONPA
OF
VILLAGE TINNO

ZONG GONPA
OF
VILLAGE TINNO

Edited by
Tobdan

Kaveri Books
New Delhi - 110 002

First Published in 2019
ISBN : 978-81-7479-224-2

Published by
Kaveri Books
4832/24, Ansari Road,
Daryaganj, New Delhi - 110 002 (India)
Ph. : 011-2328 8140, 2324 5799
E-mail : kaveribooks@vsnl.com
kaveribooks@gmail.com
Website : www.kaveribooks.com

Typesetting at Creative Graphics, Delhi

PRINTED IN INDIA

Preface

Some facts collected about the village of Tinno and its monastery, Zong Gonpa, have been presented in the book for the benefit of the visitors to the village, its inhabitants and all those who are interested. A traditional ceremonial song entitled Lha-rgyas, which is sung in the Losar (lo-gsar), New Year Festival, all over sTod, is also appended.

Tobdan

Contents

1

तिन्नो-गाँव का संक्षिप्त परिचय

ठिन्ले शाशनी

तिन्नो-गाँव, हिमाचल प्रदेश के जिला लाहुल एवं स्पिति के मुख्यालय केलंग से 14 किलोमीटर की दूरी पर स्थित है। यह गाँव मनाली-लेह मार्ग पर भागा नदी, जो सूरज-ताल सरोवर से निकलती है, के वाम तट पर समुद्र-तल से 3200 मीटर की ऊँचाई पर स्थित है। वर्ष 2011 की जनगणना के अनुसार, इस गाँव में 29 परिवार निवास कर रहे हैं। इस गाँव की जन-संख्या 125 लोगों की है, जिनमें से 59 पुरुष व 66 महिलायें हैं। गाँव की साक्षरता दर 82.35 प्रतिशत है। इस गाँव के सभी निवासी बौद्ध-धर्म के अनुयायी हैं।

ज़ोङ्-गोन्पा का वर्णन

यह गोन्पा, गाँव से कुछ ही दूरी पर पहाड़ की कन्दरा में अत्यन्त रमणीक स्थल पर स्थित है। इस गोन्पा की ऐतिहासिक जानकारी उपलब्ध नहीं है, इसलिए इसकी प्राचीनता जनश्रुति पर ही आधारित है। इस गोन्पा का दायित्व गेमुर-गोन्पा के भिक्षु-संघ के अधीन है। इसलिए, इनके द्वारा इस गोन्पा में पुजारी का चयन तीन वर्षों के लिए किया जाता है। यहाँ साधना हेतु एक अलग कक्ष भी उपलब्ध है। यह गोन्पा साधकों के लिए अत्यन्त अनुकूल स्थल है। इसलिए, कई दशकों तक स्थानीय लामा लोग अपनी साधना हेतु इस गोन्पा का उपयोग करते आ रहे हैं। यद्यपि, आज साधकों की कमी है, फिर भी, इच्छुक साधक इस गोन्पा में साधना की सिद्धि हेतु आने को आतुर रहते हैं। इस गोन्पा में गुरु पद्मसंभव, आर्य-अवलोकितेश्वर, तथा महायोगी एवं सिद्ध मिला-रेपा आदि की मूर्त्तियाँ विभिन्न मुद्राओं में प्रतिष्ठित हैं। इन मूर्त्तियों की निर्माणशैली विशिष्ट है, जिनका शिल्प-अध्ययन अपेक्षित है। यहाँ पर दीपदान हेतु एक ही पत्थर पर

108 दीयों को प्रज्वलित करने की सुविधा उपलब्ध है। प्रस्तर-कला में निपुण किसी व्यक्ति का यह अनुपम देन प्रतीत होता है। पहाड़ की कन्दरा में निर्मित इस गोन्पा में जल की व्यवस्था इसी पहाड़ से निकलने वाले चश्मे (=जल-स्रोत) से की जाती है। जब कभी भी जल-स्रोत कम हो जाता है, तब धूप (=साङ्) से धूपितकर, शुद्धिकरण करने पर जल का स्रोत बढ़ने लगता है। इस जल को औषधीय गुणों से युक्त माना जाता है। ऐसी मान्यता है कि श्रद्धा पूर्वक इस जल का आँखों में छिड़काव करने से आँखों में ताज़गी तथा रोशनी में वृद्धि होती है। इस जल की विशिष्टता यह है कि कई दिनों तक रखने पर भी यह खराब नहीं होता है। इस गोन्पा के प्रांगण के समीप देवदार (=जुनिपर) का एक विशाल हरा-भरा वृक्ष है, जो लगभग 300 वर्ष पुराना माना जाता है।

तिन्नो-गाँव के तीन विशिष्ट एवं सम्मानित व्यक्तियों के व्यक्तित्व एवं कृतित्व का संक्षिप्त परिचय

श्रद्धेय अमची ज्ञालछन (बोकरपा) : आप का जन्म वर्ष उन्नीस सौ बयालीस (1942 ई.?) में गाँव तिन्नो में हुआ। आप अत्यन्त मृदुभाषी, सहज, सरल एवं व्यवहारशील व्यक्तित्व के धनी हैं। निस्संदेह, अमची ज्ञालछन जी का व्यक्तित्व सिद्धों की चर्या से अनुप्राणित हैं। आपके पिता स्वर्गीय श्री अंगरूप छेरिंग जी भी खानदानी अमची (=सोआ-रिग्पा चिकित्सक) एवं बौद्ध-विद्याओं के प्रकाण्ड विद्वान् थे। विशेषकर, बौद्धतन्त्र-विद्या के विधि-विधानों में निपुण एवं उच्चकोटि के साधक थे। इन्होंने 18 वर्षों तक गेमुर-गोन्पा के वज्राचार्य (=दोर्जे-लोपोन) के पद को सुशोभित किया। श्रद्धेय अमची ज्ञालछ्न के बड़े भाई स्वर्गीय श्री नवांग तोबदन जी भी अमची (=सोआ-रिग्पा चिकित्सक), तान्त्रिक विधि-विधानों के विशेषज्ञ एवं साधक के रूप में प्रसिद्ध थे। इन्होंने भी गेमुर-गोन्पा के वज्राचार्य-पद को सुशोभित किया।

इस तरह, श्रद्धेय अमची ज्ञालछन जी को भोट-चिकित्सा (=सोआ-रिग्पा) एवं बौद्धतान्त्रिक-विद्याओं की पारिवारिक-परम्परा में अध्ययन करने का सौभाग्य प्राप्त हुआ, जिसके फलस्वरूप आपने अपने को उच्च कोटि का चिकित्सक एवं साधक के रूप में प्रतिष्ठित किया। आपने अपने पिता जी एवं अग्रज के अतिरिक्त तोदघाटी के गेमुर नामक गाँव के प्रसिद्ध सिद्ध एवं साधक श्रद्धेय त्रिमा नमज्ञल जी के सानिध्य में रहकर बौद्धतन्त्र-विद्याओं का अध्ययन किया। इन्हीं सद्गुरुओं

के मार्गदर्शन से आपने युवा अवस्था में ही जोङ्-गोन्पा आदि अनेक साधना-स्थलों में वर्षों तक साधना कर शमक (=चोद्) तथा श्मशानादि गुह्य साधनाओं में सिद्धि प्राप्त की।

कालान्तर में, आपने कर्ग्युद्-परम्परा के सिद्ध एवं आचार्य श्रद्धेय अफो रिन्पोछे, श्रद्धेय खेनचे़ रिन्पोछे तथा श्रद्धेय तगना रिन्पोछे आदि सद्गुरुओं से विभिन्न तन्त्र-साधनाओं के अववाद, अभिषेक एवं उपदेश प्राप्त किये। इनके अतिरिक्त, तिब्बत के खम प्रान्त के नाङ्-छेन नामक स्थान से पधारे सिद्धाचार्य श्रद्धेय पेमा उमजे़द् जी से पतलीकुहल में आकस्मिक मुलाकात के उपरान्त, आपने उन्हें महान् सिद्ध एवं बौद्ध अध्यात्म-विद्या के ज्ञाता के रूप में जाना। आपने इस आकस्मिक-मिलन को पूर्वजन्म का संयोग एवं पुण्य का फल माना और उन्हें सद्गुरु के रूप में स्वीकार किया। आपने निरन्तर कई वर्षों तक उनके सानिध्य में रहकर तन्त्र के विभिन्न गुह्य-साधनाओं एवं विधि-विधानों से सम्बद्ध अववाद एवं उपदेश प्राप्त किया। आप अपने को भाग्यशाली मानते हैं कि ऐसे महान् साधक के साथ आपका मिलन हुआ, जिसके कारण आपको अपने आध्यात्मिक-ज्ञान का विकास करने का सु-अवसर प्राप्त हुआ।

28 वर्ष की युवावस्था में आप तिन्नों गाँव से स्थानान्तरित होकर डोभी आ गये। विगत 48 वर्षों से आप गाँव शिम, डाकघर डोभी, ज़िला कुल्लु में निवास कर रहे हैं। तब से लेकर आजतक, कुल्लु ज़िले में निवास कर रहे लाहुलियों एवं स्थानीय कुल्लु-वासियों के हित के लिए तथागत बुद्ध के मानवीय मूल्यों से प्रेरित होकर, निःस्वार्थ-सेवाभाव से अपनी चिकित्सा-विद्या एवं तान्त्रिक-अनुष्ठानों के माध्यम से लोक-कल्याण करने में तत्पर हैं। साथ ही साथ, आपके पास आने वाले समस्त लोगों को बौद्धधर्म के प्रति जागरुक भी करते हैं। इस तरह आपकी ख्याति सम्पूर्ण कुल्लु घाटी में फैली हुई है। निस्संदेह, आप बोधिसत्त्व की चर्या का जीवन-यापन करते हैं। आपने अपने सम्पूर्ण जीवन को करुणा से द्रवित होकर, सांसारिक-दुःखों से पीड़ित लोगों के हित के लिए समर्पित कर दिया है। परम पावन दलाई-लामा जी ने भी एक प्रवचन के अवसर पर, आपके करुणाशील व्यक्तित्व को अनुभवकर, सभा में मौजूद हजारों अनुयायियों की उपस्थिति में आशीर्वाद प्रदान किया है। इसी प्रकार, श्रद्धेय छोगोन रिन्पोछे आदि महानुभावों ने

भी आपके सत्कृत्य एवं करुणाशील व्यक्तित्व से प्रभावित होकर आशीर्वाद प्रदान किये हैं।

समस्त तिनो गाँववासी आपके इस लोक-कल्याण के प्रति समर्पण एवं बौद्ध-धर्म के प्रति महान् योगदान के लिए गर्व महसूस करते हैं तथा तथागत बुद्ध से आपके दीर्घजीवी होने की कामना करते हैं।

श्रद्धेय नवांग रिगजिन (फिमा) : आपका जन्म गाँव तिन्नो में हुआ। आपने आरम्भिक शिक्षा वाराणसी संस्कृत विश्वविद्यालय में, परम श्रद्धेय खुनु लामा तेन्जिन ग्यलछन जैसे बोधिसत्त्व के चरणों में रहकर प्राप्त की। किन्हीं कारणों से आप अधिक समय तक वाराणसी में अध्ययन हेतु नहीं रह सके। वहाँ से लौटने के पश्चात् आपने बौद्धधर्म का स्व-अध्ययन जारी रखा। आपकी विशेष रुचि भोट-व्याकरण, संस्कृत-भोटशब्दावलि, स्तूप-निर्माण तथा काष्ठ-कला एवं थंका-चित्रण आदि में हैं। इन विद्याओं से सम्बद्ध अनेक भोट एवं संस्कृत ग्रन्थों का भी आपने संग्रह किया है। इनके अतिरिक्त, भोट-बौद्धधर्म-दर्शन एवं भोट-साहित्य से सम्बद्ध भोट एवं संस्कृत-शास्त्रों के संकलन में भी आपकी गहरी रुचि है, जिसके फलस्वरूप आपने अपने घर में क-ग्युर एवं तन्-ग्युर सहित अनेक बौद्धधर्म के भोट एवं संस्कृत साहित्यों का संकलन किया है। आप बहु-आयामी व्यक्तित्व के धनी हैं। आप ने तोदघाटी के लाहुली संस्कृति के संरक्षण में विशेषकर, शादी-विवाहों में गाये जाने वाले पारम्परिक लोक-गीतों के संरक्षण एवं संवर्द्धन में अपना अमूल्य योगदान दिया है। आप तोद-घाटी में शादी-विवाह के अवसर पर लु-पोन (प्रधान-गायक) के रूप में प्रसिद्ध हैं। इसके अतिरिक्त स्तूप-निर्माण में आपकी विशेष दक्षता है। पूरे लाहुल एवं पंगी घाटी में आप ही ऐसे शख्सीयत हैं, जो विधि-विधान पूर्वक स्तूप निर्माण करने में सक्षम हैं। आपके इस महान् एवं उल्लेखनीय योगदान के लिए, 16 अगस्त, 2003 को तत्कालीन लाहुल-स्पिति के जिलाधीश महोदय ने आपको सम्मान-पत्र प्रदान किया है। आपने भी गेमुर गोन्पा के वज्राचार्य पद को सुशोभित किया है। आपने लाहुल एवं पंगी घाटी में अनेक स्तूपों का निर्माण किये हैं। आपने अपने गाँव में भी गाँव-वालों के आर्थिक-सहयोग से एक मणिचक्र एवं स्तूप का भी निर्माण किये हैं। इनके अतिरिक्त, आपने गाँव में ही अपने संसाधनों से खोआ-नामक स्थान पर स्तूप का निर्माण किया है, जो तिन्नो-गाँव के वातावरण को अत्यन्त

धार्मिक एवं सुरम्य बनाता है। हम तिन्नो-गाँववासी आपके बहु-आयामी व्यक्तित्व के प्रति सम्मान व्यक्त करते हुए तथागत बुद्ध से दीर्घायु की कामना करते हैं।

श्री तोबदन (तेनखंगपा) : भाषाविद्, लेखक, चिन्तक एवं हिमालयी-संस्कृति के विशेषज्ञ श्री तोबदन जी का जन्म वर्ष 1945 में हुआ। आपने अथक परिश्रम से अपनी शिक्षा सरकारी विद्यालयों एवं कालेजों से पूर्ण करने के उपरान्त रिज़र्ब-बैंक के अन्तर्गत संचालित नावार्ड बैंक में सरकारी नौकरी प्राप्त की। अपने कार्य के प्रति अत्यन्त निष्ठा एवं दायित्व के निर्वहन के फलस्वरूप उच्च-पद पर आसीन होकर, सेवानिवृत हुये। सरकारी सेवा में रहते हुए भी आपने अध्ययन के प्रति रुचि बरकरार रखी, जिसके फलस्वरूप आपके कई ग्रन्थ प्रकाशित हुये। सरकारी दायित्वों को निभाते हुए अध्ययन के प्रति गहन रुचि रखने वाले लोग विरले ही होते हैं। इससे यह सिद्ध होता है कि आप कितने अधिक विद्या-अनुराग्री हैं। आज की नयी पीढ़ी के लिए आप प्रेरणा के स्रोत हैं। नावार्ड से सेवा-निवृत्ति के उपरान्त, आपने अपने जीवन को लाहुल एवं इसके समीपवर्ती क्षेत्रों के सांस्कृतिक, धार्मिक एवं ऐतिहासिक अध्ययन के लिए समर्पित कर दिया है। आप अंग्रेजी, हिन्दी एवं भोटी इन तीनों भाषाओं में ग्रन्थों की रचना करते हैं। आपका अध्ययन-क्षेत्र विशेषकर भोटी-भाषा, सामाजिक-रीति-रिवाज़ों, धार्मिक-क्रियाओं तथा इतिहास से सम्बद्ध हैं। आपने इन विषयों से सम्बद्ध अनेक ग्रन्थ प्रकाशित किये हैं, जिसके फलस्वरूप आप की रचनाओं को न केवल हिमाचल में, अपितु देश-विदेश में भी प्रतिष्ठा मिली है। दिनांक 3 अगस्त, 2017 को इण्डिया इन्टरनेशनल सेन्टर, नई दिल्ली में *People's Linguistic Survey of India (PLSI)* के द्वारा 11 खण्डों में प्रकाशित ग्रन्थों के विमोचन के अवसर पर हिमाचल-प्रदेश खण्ड के अंग्रेजी-संस्करण के सम्पादन हेतु भूतपूर्व प्रधानमन्त्री डॉ. मनमोहन सिंह जी के कर-कमलों से आपको सम्मानितकर मान बढ़ाया है। आपकी विद्वता, अध्ययनशीलता एवं कर्मनिष्ठता ने तिन्नो-गाँव को सम्मानित किया है। हम सभी ग्रामवासी गर्व महसूस करते हैं, तथा आपकी दीर्घायु की कामना करते हैं। आपके द्वारा अबतक प्रकाशित ग्रन्थों की सूची निम्नलिखित हैं-

1. History and Religion of *Lahul,* (1984).
2. The People of the Upper Valley (sTodpas of *Lahul* in the Himalayas, (1993).

3. Historical documents from Trans-Himalayan *Lahul, Zanskar* and *Ladakh*, (Co-Author) with C. Dorje, (1996).
4. *Kullu* A Historical Study (2000)
5. Moravian Missionaries in the Trans-Western Himalayas, Co-Author with C. Dorje, (2008).
6. *Bashahar Kinnaur:* A Study in Cultural History of Western Trans-Himalaya, (2008).
7. Exploring *Malana* (2011).
8. Bhoti Paricaya Vyakaran Aur Anubad in Hindi and Bhoti (1990).
9. A Grammar of sTodpa Language, (2015).

श्रद्धेय भट्टारक छोगोन रिन्पोछे जी का संक्षिप्त परिचय

परम श्रद्धेय तेन्जिन छोकी ज्ञाछो (छोगोन रिन्पोछे) जी डुग्पा-कर्ग्युद् सम्प्रदाय के महान् प्रचारकों में से एक हैं। आप सोलहवीं सदी के डुग्पा-कर्ग्युद् सम्प्रदाय के महान् सिद्धाचार्य **थूछेन छोकी गोन्यो (1501-1582 ई.)** के नवें अवतार (=निर्माणकाय-धारी) हैं, जो बोधिसत्त्व वज्रपाणि की परम्परा में अवतरित हैं तथा महान् भोटाचार्य पद्मा-करपो (1527-1592 ई.) के गुरु हैं। आप तिब्बत स्थित पल-देछेन-छोखोर-लिङ् मठ के मठाधीश हैं। महामहिम 14वें दलाई लामा जी के निर्देशन में आपकी खोज **छोगोन रिन्पोछे** के रूप में लद्दाख में हुई। तत्पश्चात्, परम श्रद्धेय गुरु गा रिन्पोछे के नेतृत्व में रारंग टशी-छोलिङ् मठ में आपका पीठाभिषेक हुआ। वर्तमान में, आपने पल-देछेन छोखोर-लिङ् नाम से देहरादून, उत्तराखण्ड में अपना केन्द्रीय मठ स्थापित किया है। सम्प्रति, लदाख तथा किन्नौर में भी इस मठ की शाखायें स्थापित हैं। आपकी आरम्भिक शिक्षा रारंग, (किन्नौर) एवं देहरादून में सम्पन्न हुई। आपने अपनी उच्च-शिक्षा धर्मशाला स्थित इन्स्टीच्यूट ऑफ बुद्धिस्ट डॉयलेक्टीक्स से पूर्ण की। आप विगत तीन दशकों से किन्नौर घाटी में बौद्ध धर्म के प्रचार-प्रसार में सतत प्रयत्नशील हैं। आप प्रतिवर्ष लदाख तथा किन्नौर के स्थानीय लोगों को मन्त्र-जाप साधना एवं अपने प्रवचनों के माध्यम से बौद्धधर्म की शिक्षाओं को प्रदान करते आ रहे हैं। इस घाटी के लोगों के लिए आपका योगदान अतुलनीय है।

तिन्नो-गाँव के तत्वावधान में सम्पन्न धार्मिक-अनुष्ठान कार्यक्रम

दिनांक 8 जून, 2018 को परम श्रद्धेय छोगोन रिन्पोछे जी के आगमन पर गाँववालों ने सम्मानपूर्वक परम्परागत–रीति से उनका स्वागत किया। तत्पश्चात, दिनांक 9 जून, 2018 को गाँव–वालों के अनुदान से निर्मित्त शि़ठो–दम्पा रिगस–ग्या–थंका (=शान्त–रौद्र शतकुल देव–पट्टचित्र) का रब–ने (=प्राण–प्रतिष्ठा)–अनुष्ठान परम श्रद्धेय भट्टारक छोगोन रिन्पोछे तेन्जिन छोकी ज्ञाछो़ जी के कर–कमलों से सम्पन्न हुआ। इसी दिन रिन्पोछे जी ने गाँव के प्रत्येक घर में जाकर घर एवं परिवार की सुख–समृद्धि एवं शान्ति हेतु मंगल–कामना की तथा बुद्ध एवं बोधिसत्त्वों से सर्व–कल्याण हेतु प्रार्थना की। उसी के अगले दिन, दिनांक 10 जून को रिन्पोछे जी ने गाँव में आमन्त्रित समस्त श्रद्धालुजनों को छे़–वङ् तथा छे़–डुब (दीर्घायु–अभिषेक) से अभिषिक्त कर आशीर्वाद प्रदान किया। इस प्रकार, गाँव वालों ने इस मंगल कार्य को सम्पन्न करने हेतु रिन्पोछे जी के प्रति श्रद्धा–सुमन एवं आभार व्यक्त किया तथा सम्मानपूर्वक परम्परागत–रीति से विदाई दी। इसतरह गाँव के समस्त लोगों के सत्प्रयास से यह मंगल–कार्यक्रम सफलतापूर्वक सम्पन्न हुआ।

।। भवतु सर्वमंगलम्।।

• • •

2
Monastery of Zong Gonpa Tinno

Tobdan

Tinno is a small village of about twenty households where there reside about 200 souls and is situated in the traditional geographical-cultural set up of sTod, the Upper region of river Bhaga, at a distance of about sixteen kilometers from Kyelang, the headquarters of district Lahul-Spiti, towards north, on the Kyelang-Leh highway. It is situated on a flat plateau, on the left bank of Bhaga river, deep below at the foot of the high rising hill, across Karing. Therefore in the society of sTodpa, the other sTodpas, the village has been assigned a nickname as Adu-Kodong (Potato Pit = A pit dug up in the fields below under the ground in which potato is preserved in the winter). Its most natural distinctive feature is that the village is endowed with abundant supply of water, a matter of envy for many villages in Lahul. Two vast streams flow down from its two sides: Muntsi dokpo on the north-east, towards Jispa and Tsapor dokpo on the south-east, towards Chugta. In olden times till some years after the Independence around 1960 the village was connected with the world on the other side of the river by a rope bridge of birchwood branches known as shika-zampa. It was repaired every year by the collective labour of the villagers.

Tinno is connected by the mountain pass with Sra-srin, in Tinan valley, where presently there is the temple of Gepang, on the side of Gondhla of the Sissu stream, and Khwagling, on the side of Khoksar, both now called Sissu. From Tinno one climbs up just above the village slightly to the right on the right side of Tsapor dokpo. The top of the pass on this side of the dokpo, the side of village, is called Dangra and the other side as Shurbun. Cattle are taken for grazing to Dangra and this place is rich in medicinal herbs. Thakur Dunichand of Srasrin tells that his uncle used to revere a god named Tinno Manchhod. He prepared an effigy of a goat of flour and, a bow and arrow, of willow branch.

The village has an ancient monastery named Zong (rdsong) Gonpa, fort monastery, built in a rock cave. It lies above the village about a kilometer away towards north-east. According to Lama Gyaltshan there is a legend narrating the manner of founding of the monastery in the village that two monasteries were founded in the village which are named as Zong Gonpa and Pala (Pa-la) Gonpa. These were founded by two old men named Zong meme and Pala Meme. Pala Gonpa is situated slightly above the village on a ridge towards south east of the village, just above the fields named *Rasta-tsi*, and presently it is in ruins. It is said to have been destroyed in a natural calamity. The site is still intact, unencroached by any greedy grabber, perhaps because there is no water for irrigation.. The walls of the foundation of the building stand above the ground and the area is surrounded by big juniper trees. From the ruins of the structure it is observed that in the built up area of about 90 square feet there were four rooms and a passage in the middle. Earlier the houses of the households named Bokarpa and Kyelangpa of the village also were located there, says Lama Gyaltshan Bokarpa. Gonpapa had their house at Kho-'a. In 1868 there was a household named Pharma in Tinno which became extinct.

Zong Gonpa lies in a rock cave above the fields named *Tshog-dang*. Earlier the building was of two storeys. Some pillars of the structure got rotten and the monastery crumbled down. Now it is of one storey. There are four statues all of clay in the temple: on the left of the viewer is that of Avalokitesvara, in the middle are two statues of Guru Rinpochhe i.e. Padmasambhava and on the right is of Mila Repa. Of the two statues of Guru the larger one belongs to the monastery itself and the smaller one is said to have been brought from Pala Gonpa, narrates Lama Gyaltshan. The other two were made afterwards. It is told that the narration containing the story of foundation of the monastery (chhags-rabs) is contained in a book in the monastery of Zonkhul in Zanskar. Pala Meme and Zong Meme were envious of each other. If one lama was called for worship ceremony in a household, *torma,* the sacrificial effigies, were thrown towards the direction of the other.

The monastery has two regular officials. dKon-gnyer, the lama priest, is appointed for a period of three years by the monastic organization of Gemur Gonpa, which overlooks all the monasteries in whole of sTod valley. The regular mchhod-gnas, the lay person who lights lamps and attends to some other small chores in the monastery is appointed by the villagers for a period of three years. Norbu is presently mchhod-gnas of the monastery, who belongs to the traditional class of craftsman of iron who were not assigned such kind of works earlier.

Every year in the month of June white-washing of the building is done called dkar-rtsis (white-paint) in which locally obtained white earth is painted. One person comes from each household for the service. Prayer lamps are lighted everyday. There may be defaults during the period of heavy snowfall. A worship is held occasionally called gsol-ka. A big prayer called Zong Tshe-shu (bchu) is held every year on the fixed day of 10th day of 6th month of Tibetan calendar, about in August. This date is considered as the date of birth of the Guru. But it is observed that the date of celebration of the occasion varies. While the date remains at all places the same as the tenth the month varies from place to place. Here ii is held in the sixth month, at Riwalsar in Mandi it is held in the first month and at other places it is held in the fifth month of the Tibetan calendar.

The monastery is in possession of a unique object called Gyam-mchhod (brgya-mchhod = hundred worship lamps, actually 108). It is a round circular flat stone slab of diameter of about one and half feet. On it is carved in concentric circles ridges and drains alternately with one hundred and eight holes for lighting the worship lamps. Oil can be put in it at one place and it spreads uniformly to all the lamps itself. It is still used sometimes. Such objects are seen at very few places in Lahul. There are one big and one small gyam-chhod at Rangtsa, on the pass between Kardang and Gondhla. The slabs are square and in them there are only holes and oil has to be poured in the individual hole. In the bigger slab the holes may number 108. These are not in use presently. It is told that similar multi-lamp stone slab existed at Riwalsar in Mandi. This is one of the signs indicating antiquity of the monastery.

Gyaltshan tells further that earlier there used to be held the festival of Tshe-shu, in which mask dance was held. This is held as the Padmasambhava's birthday. The people of village Melang used to come to see the festival walking along the river Bhaga and stayed at Tshog-dang in the fields near the monastery. They wore a cap named Baltib (cap from Baltistan). The Melang village which is now called Zemug was a village of one hundred households. Once there came an old lady in the village. In the gathering of the villagers she was not given any importance and she was placed in the last in the row in the sitting. But one of the observers sensed some importance and took her to sit at the head of the row. In the night the portion of the hill above the village fell down over the village and buried the whole village under its debris and killed all the villagers. But the man who had given place at the head of the row to the old woman was thrown away by the force of wind to the other side of the river and was saved. This house is presently known as Lumpa Champa (Lungpho byungpo = the spirit of wind). The ruins of the village situated near Dartse just below the junction of rivers on the bank on the right side of the river is wholly covered by the big boulders of splintered rocks and is named as Zemug. It is also told by some people that some articles like broken wood pieces sometimes become exposed near the river as it eats up the edges of the ruins. At present there is no sign of any kind in the monastery indicting the existence of the tradition of mask dance if ever it was held here.

Here there is a small source of water. It drips from the crevices of the rock and is collected below. It is told that when smoke is made below the rock the flow of the water increases. The water is sufficient for use here even when sometimes some ceremonies are held. The monastery is in possession of land. This is also recorded in the Settlement report of 1868.

From all the artifacts existing in the monastery it may be assumed that the monastery was originally founded in the tradition of Nyingma, Ancient tradition, dedicated to the Guru, including that of Pala Gonpa. Both the statues of the Guru are original. There are small old books containing prayers to the Guru like Le'u bdunma. But they are incomplete.

One important book, na-ra-ga dong sprugs rnal-'byor gyi spyi-khrus, containing only the first and the last leaves, is co-authored by Guru Padmasambhava with Vimal Mitra of Kashmir and translated into Tibetan by Jyana Kumar and Mani Nachhen Chhog. According to Rahul Sankrityayan the former three are contemporary, (Rahul Sankrityayan: 1948: Appendix-9, sa).

Presently as the villagers exhibit themselves, it is gzhung-'brug of 'brug-pa sect. Similar rock embedded monasteries in Lahul are situated at Beeling (Yurzong gonpa) and Khoksar.

Reference

Rahul Sankrityayan. (1948). *Tibbat me bauddh dharma*, second edition, 1979, Kitab Mahal, Illahabad.

• • •

3
Lha-rgyas

Tobdan

III ལྷ་རྒྱས། Lha-rgyas

༄༅། །དང་པོ་ལ་བཀྲ་ཤིས།

༄༅། །དང་པོ་ལ་བཀྲ་ཤིས་ཡོང་ཤིག། ལ་དཀྱུང་ལ་ཞེབས་སོང་།
ཡོང་ཤིག། ལ་ཡོང་ཤིག་དཀྱུང་ལ། དཀྱུང་ལ་ས་བཀྲ་ཤིས་ཡོང་ཤིག།
ལ་མི་དེ་ནང་དུ་ཡོང་ཤིག། ལ་ཡོང་ཤིག་མི་དེ།
ཁྲི་དུ་དཀྱིལ་ལ་བཞུགས་ས། ཡོང་ཤིག་ལ་དཀྱུང་སྟོད་དཀྱིལ་དུ།
ཡོང་ཤིག། ལ་ཡོང་ཤིག། དཀྱུང་སྟོད་དཀྱིལ་ལ་བཞུགས་ས་ལ་ཞེབས་སོང་།
ཡོང་ཤིག། ལ་བཀྲ་ཤིས་བརྗོད།། –1

དང་པོ་ལ་བཀྲ་ཤིས་ཡོང་ཤིག། ལ་གངས་ལ་ཞེབས་སོང་།
ཡོང་ཤིག། ལ་ཡོང་ཤིག་གངས་ལ། གངས་ལ་ས་བཀྲ་ཤིས་ཡོང་ཤིག།།
ལ་མི་དེ་ནང་དུ། ཡོང་ཤིག། ལ་ཡོང་ཤིག་མི་དེ་
སེང་ཆེན་གྱི་ལ་བཞུགས་ས། ཡོང་ཤིག་ལ་གངས་སྟོད་དཀྱིལ་དུ།
ཡོང་ཤིག། ལ་ཡོང་ཤིག། གངས་སྟོད་དཀྱིལ་ལ་བཞུགས་ས་ལ་ཞེབས་སོང་།
ཡོང་ཤིག། ལ་བཀྲ་ཤིས་བརྗོད།།–2

དང་པོ་ལ་བཀྲ་ཤིས་ཡོང་ཤིག། ལ་ནགས་ལ་ཞེབས་སོང་།
ཡོང་ཤིག། ལ་ཡོང་ཤིག་ནགས་ལ། ནགས་ལ་ས་བཀྲ་ཤིས་ཡོང་ཤིག།
ལ་མི་དེ་ནང་དུ་ཡོང་ཤིག། ལ་ཡོང་ཤིག་མི་དེ།
སྟག་ཆེན་གྱི་ལ་བཞུགས་ས། ཡོང་ཤིག་ལ་ནགས་སྟོད་དཀྱིལ་དུ།
ཡོང་ཤིག། ལ་ཡོང་ཤིག། ནགས་སྟོད་དཀྱིལ་ལ་བཞུགས་ས་ལ་ཞེབས་སོང་།
ཡོང་ཤིག། ལ་བཀྲ་ཤིས་བརྗོད།། –3

དང་པོ་ལ་བཀྲ་ཤིས་ཡོང་ཤིག། ལ་མཚོ་ལ་ཕེབས་སོང་།

ཡོང་ཤིག། ལ་ཡོང་ཤིག་མཚོ་ལ། མཚོ་ལ་མ་བཀྲིས་ཡོང་ཤིག།

ལ་མི་དེ་ནང་དུ་ཡོང་ཤིག། ལ་ཡོང་ཤིག་མི་དེ།

ཉ་ཆེན་གྱི་ལ་བཞུགས་ས། ཡོང་ཤིག་ལ་མཚོ་སྟོད་དཀྱིལ་དུ།

ཡོང་ཤིག། ལ་ཡོང་ཤིག། མཚོ་སྟོད་དཀྱིལ་ལ་བཞུགས་ས་ལ་ཕེབས་སོང་།

ཡོང་ཤིག། ལ་བཀྲ་ཤིས་བརྗོད།། --4

དང་པོ་ལ་བཀྲ་ཤིས་ཡོང་ཤིག། ལ་མཁར་ལ་ཕེབས་སོང་།

ཡོང་ཤིག། ལ་ཡོང་ཤིག་མཁར་ལ། མཁར་ལ་མ་བཀྲིས་ཡོང་ཤིག།

ལ་མི་དེ་ནང་དུ་ཡོང་ཤིག། ལ་ཡོང་ཤིག་མི་དེ།

མི་ཆེན་གྱི་ལ་བཞུགས་ས། ཡོང་ཤིག་ལ་མཁར་སྟོད་དཀྱིལ་དུ།

ཡོང་ཤིག། ལ་ཡོང་ཤིག། མཁར་སྟོད་དཀྱིལ་ལ་བཞུགས་ས་ལ་ཕེབས་སོང་།

ཡོང་ ཤིག། ལ་བཀྲ་ཤིས་བརྗོད།། --5

དང་པོ་ལ་བཀྲ་ཤིས་ཡོང་ཤིག། ལ་དཔལ་ལ་ཕེབས་སོང་།

ཡོང་ཤིག། ལ་ཡོང་ཤིག་དཔལ་ལ། དཔལ་ལ་མ་བཀྲ་ཤིས་ཡོང་ཤིག།

ལ་མི་དེ་ནང་དུ་ཡོང་ཤིག། ལ་ཡོང་ཤིག་མི་དེ།

ཡབ་ཡུམ་གྱི་ལ་བཞུགས་ས། ཡོང་ཤིག་ལ་དཔལ་ཁང་སྟོད་དཀྱིལ་དུ།

ཡོང་ཤིག། ལ་ཡོང་ཤིག། དཔལ་སྟོད་དཀྱིལ་ལ་བཞུགས་ས་ལ་ཕེབས་སོང་།

ཡོང་ཤིག། ལ་བཀྲ་ཤིས་བརྗོད།། --6

༄༅།།༢།།གཉིས་པ་འཛོམ་སྐྱ།།

༄༅།། དགུང་སྟོད་དུ་བཞུགས་པའི། ཁྲི་གདུགས་ཉི་མ་བདེ།།

དགུང་སྨད་དུ་བཞུགས་པའི། དཀར་གསལ་ཟླ་བ་བདེ།

དགུང་སྟོད་དཀྱིལ་དུ་འཛོམ་པའི། རྒྱུ་སྐར་འཛོམ་པོ་བདེ། །
དེ་ནས་གཅིག་དང་གཉིས་གསུམ། འཛོམ་པའི་ཆ་གཅིག་དགོས།
ཏ་ལི་ཡང་ལ་ལ། ལ་ལི་བཀྲ་ཤིས་བརྗོད། --1

གངས་སྟོད་དུ་བཞུགས་པའི།། སེང་ཆེན་དཀར་མོ་བདེ།།
གངས་སྨད་དུ་བཞུགས་པའི།། གཡུ་རལ་ལེགས་མོ་བདེ།
གངས་སྟོད་དཀྱིལ་དུ་འཛོམས་པའི།། སེང་ཕྲུག་འཛོམ་པོ་བདེ།།
དེ་ནས་གཅིག་དང་གཉིས་གསུམ །།འཛོམ་པའི་ཆ་གཅིག་དགོས།།།
ཏ་ལི་ཡང་ལ་ལ། ལ་ལི་བཀྲ་ཤིས་བརྗོད། --2

ནགས་སྟོད་དུ་བཞུགས་པའི།། སྟག་ཆེན་ཁྲ་བོ་བདེ།
ནགས་སྨད་དུ་བཞུགས་པའི།། རི་མོ་ལེགས་མོ་བདེ།།
ནགས་སྟོད་དཀྱིལ་དུ་འཛོམ་པའི།། སྟག་ཕྲུག་འཛོམ་པོ་བདེ།།
དེ་ནས་གཅིག་དང་གཉིས་གསུམ།། འཛོམ་པའི་ཆ་གཅིག་དགོས།།
ཏ་ལི་ཡང་ལ་ལ། ལ་ལི་བཀྲ་ཤིས་བརྗོད། --3

མཚོ་སྟོད་དུ་བཞུགས་པའི།། ཉ་ཆེན་ཞུལ་མོ་བདེ།།
མཚོ་སྨད་དུ་བཞུགས་པའི།། གསེར་མིག་ལེགས་མོ་བདེ།།
མཚོ་སྟོད་དཀྱིལ་དུ་འཛོམ་པའི།། ཉ་ཕྲུག་འཛོམ་པོ་བདེ།།
དེ་ནས་གཅིག་དང་གཉིས་གསུམ། འཛོམ་པའི་ཆ་གཅིག་དགོས།
ཏ་ལི་ཡང་ལ་ལ། ལ་ལི་བཀྲ་ཤིས་བརྗོད།། --4

མཁར་སྟོད་དུ་བཞུགས་པའི། མི་ཆེན་གོང་མ་བདེ།
མཁར་སྨད་དུ་བཞུགས་པའི། རྒྱུད་རིས་མཐོན་པོ་བདེ།
མཁར་དཀྱིལ་དུ་འཛོམས་པའི། གྲོང་འཁོར་འཛོམ་པོ་བདེ།

དེ་ནས་གཅིག་དང་གཉིས་གསུམ། འཛོམ་པའི་ཆ་གཅིག་དགོས།
ཏ་ཝི་འང་ལ་ལག ལ་ཝི་བཀྲ་ཤིས་བརྗོད།། -5

དཔལ་སྟོད་དུ་བཞུགས་པའི། ཡབ་ཡུམ་པ་མ་བདེ།
དཔལ་སྨད་དུ་བཞུགས་པའི། བུ་ནོར་ཚོད་པོ་བདེ།
དཔལ་ཁང་དཀྱིལ་དུ་འཛོམ་པའི། གཉེན་དྲུང་འཛོམ་པོ་བདེ།
དེ་ནས་གཅིག་དང་གཉིས་གསུམ། འཛོམ་པའི་ཆ་གཅིག་དགོས།
ཏ་ཝི་ལ་འང་ལ་ལག ལ་ཝི་བཀྲ་ཤིས་བརྗོད།། -6

༄༅།།ཀ།། གསུམ་ཀུར་སྦུབ་ཆེ།།

༄། དཀུང་སྟོད་དཀྱིལ་དུ། ཀུར་ཞིག་སྦུབ་སོང་།
ཆེ་དང་ཆེ་ཡི། ཀུར་དེ་སྦུབ་སོང་།
སེར་པོ་དར་གྱི། ཀུར་དེ་སྦུབ་སོང་།
ཤུ་དང་ཤུ་ཡིས། ཚུགས་ཤིང་བཙུགས་སོང་།
ཁྲི་གདུགས་ཉི་མས། ཚུགས་ཤིང་བཙུགས་སོང་།
ཤུ་དང་ཤུ་ཡིས། མཚམས་ཐག་སྦུལ་སོང་།
རྒྱུ་སྐར་མང་གིས། མཚམས་ཐག་སྦུལ་སོང་།
མཚམས་ཐག་སྦུལ་བའི། བཀྲ་ཤིས་འང་བརྗོད།།-1

གངས་སྟོད་དཀྱིལ་དུ། ཀུར་ཞིག་སྦུབ་སོང་།
ཆེ་དང་ཆེ་ཡི། ཀུར་དེ་སྦུབ་སོང་།
དཀར་པོ་དར་གྱི། ཀུར་དེ་སྦུབ་སོང་།
ཤུ་དང་ཤུ་ཡིས། ཚུགས་ཤིང་བཙུགས་སོང་།
སེང་ཆེན་དཀར་མོས། ཚུགས་ཤིང་བཙུགས་སོང་།

སུ་དང་སུ་ཡིས། མཚམས་ཐག་སྤྲུལ་སོང་།
སེང་ཕྱུག་མང་གིས། མཚམས་ཐག་སྤྲུལ་སོང་།
མཚམས་ཐག་སྤྲུལ་བའི། བཀྲ་ཤིས་འང་བརྗོད།། --2

ནགས་སྟོད་དཀྱིལ་དུ། གུར་ཞིག་སྤུབ་སོང་།
ཅི་དང་ཅི་ཡི། གུར་དེ་སྤུབ་སོང་།
ཁྲ་བོ་དར་གྱི། གུར་དེ་སྤུབ་སོང་།
སུ་དང་སུ་ཡིས། ཚུགས་ཤིང་བཙུགས་སོང་།
སྟག་ཆེན་ཁྲ་བོས། ཚུགས་ཤིང་བཙུགས་སོང་།
སུ་དང་སུ་ཡིས། མཚམས་ཐག་སྤྲུལ་སོང་།
སྟག་ཕྱུག་མང་གིས། མཚམས་ཐག་སྤྲུལ་སོང་།
མཚམས་ཐག་སྤྲུལ་བའི། བཀྲ་ཤིས་འང་བརྗོད།། --3

མཚོ་སྟོད་དཀྱིལ་དུ། གུར་ཞིག་སྤུབ་སོང་།
ཅི་དང་ཅི་ཡི། གུར་དེ་སྤུབ་སོང་།
སྔོན་པོ་དར་གྱི། གུར་དེ་སྤུབ་སོང་།
སུ་དང་སུ་ཡིས། ཚུགས་ཤིང་བཙུགས་སོང་།
ཉ་ཆེན་ཁུལ་མོས། ཚུགས་ཤིང་བཙུགས་སོང་།
སུ་དང་སུ་ཡིས། མཚམས་ཐག་སྤྲུལ་སོང་།
ཉ་ཕྱུག་མང་གྱིས། མཚམས་ཐག་སྤྲུལ་སོང་།
མཚམས་ཐག་སྤྲུལ་བའི། བཀྲ་ཤིས་འང་བརྗོད།། --4

མཁར་སྟོད་དཀྱིལ་དུ། གུར་ཞིག་སྤུབ་སོང་།
ཅི་དང་ཅི་ཡི། གུར་དེ་སྤུབ་སོང་།
སེ་བོ་དར་གི། གུར་དེ་སྤུབ་སོང་།

སུ་དང་སུ་ཡིས། ཚུགས་ཤིང་བཙུགས་སོང་།
མི་ཆེན་གོང་མས། ཚུགས་ཤིང་བཙུགས་སོང་།
སུ་དང་སུ་ཡིས། མཚམས་ཐག་སྤྲུལ་སོང་།
ཀྲུང་འཁོར་མང་གྱིས། མཚམས་ཐག་སྤྲུལ་སོང་།
མཚམས་ཐག་སྤྲུལ་བའི། བཀྲ་ཤིས་འང་བརྗོད།། --5

དཔལ་སྤྱོད་དཀྱིལ་དུ། ཀུར་ཞིག་ཕུབ་སོང་།
ཅི་དང་ཅི་ཡི། ཀུར་དེ་ཕུབ་སོང་།
སྨུག་པོ་དར་གི། ཀུར་དེ་ཕུབ་སོང་།
སུ་དང་སུ་ཡིས། ཚུགས་ཤིང་བཙུགས་སོང་།
ཡབ་ཡུམ་པ་མས། ཚུགས་ཤིང་བཙུགས་སོང་།
སུ་དང་སུ་ཡིས། མཚམས་ཐག་སྤྲུལ་སོང་།
གཉེན་ཉུང་མང་གྱིས། མཚམས་ཐག་སྤྲུལ་སོང་།
མཚམས་ཐག་སྤྲུལ་བའི། བཀྲ་ཤིས་འང་བརྗོད།། --6

༄༅།།4།། བཞི་པ་ཁྲི་བཞངས་ཅེ།།

སྟོན་ཆེ་བསྐལ་པ་བཟང་པོ་ལ། ཁྲི་ཞིག་བཞངས་སོང་།
ཅི་དང་ཅི་ཡི། ཁྲི་དེ་བཞངས་སོང་།
སེར་པོ་གསེར་གྱི། ཁྲི་ཞིག་བཞངས་སོང་།
དེ་རུ་སུ་དང་། སུ་མི་བཞུགས་སོང་།
དེ་རུ་སྟེང་གི། ལྷ་ཡང་བཞུགས་སོང་།
དབུ་སྟོག་ཐོ་བའི་ལྷ། དེ་ལ་བཀྲ་ཤིས་འང་བརྗོད།། --1

སྟོན་ཆེ་བསྐལ་པ་བཟང་པོ་ལ། ཁྲི་ཞིག་བཞེངས་སོང་།

ཅི་དང་ཅི་ཡི། ཁྲི་དེ་བཞེངས་སོང་།

དཀར་པོ་དངུལ་གྱི། ཁྲི་ཞིག་བཞེངས་སོང་།

དེ་རུ་སུ་དང་། སུ་མི་བཞུགས་སོང་།

དེ་རུ་བར་གྱི། བཙན་ཡང་བཞུགས་སོང་།

གངས་རི་བཟང་པོའི་བཙན། དེ་ལ་བཀྲ་ཤིས་འང་བརྗོད།། --2

སྟོན་ཆེ་བསྐལ་པ་བཟང་པོ་ལ། ཁྲི་ཞིག་བཞེངས་སོང་།

ཅི་དང་ཅི་ཡི། ཁྲི་དེ་བཞེངས་སོང་།

སྟོན་པོ་གཡུ་ཡི། ཁྲི་ཞིག་བཞེངས་སོང་།

དེ་རུ་སུ་དང་། སུ་མི་བཞུགས་སོང་།

དེ་རུ་འོག་གི་།ཀླུ་ཡང་བཞུགས།

གཡུ་མཚོ་སྔོངས་པོའི་ཀླུ་སྨན། དེ་ལ་བཀྲ་ཤིས་འང་བརྗོད།། --3

སྟོན་ཆེ་བསྐལ་པ་བཟང་པོ་ལ། ཁྲི་ཞིག་བཞེངས་སོང་།

ཅི་དང་ཅི་ཡི། ཁྲི་དེ་བཞེངས་སོང་།

ཁྲ་བོ་ཤེལ་གྱི་ཁྲི་ཞིག་བཞེངས་སོང་།

དེ་རུ་སུ་དང་སུ་མི་བཞུགས་སོང་།

དེ་རུ་མི་ཆེན་གོང་མ་བཞུགས་སོང་།།

རྒྱུད་རིས་མཐོན་པོའི་མི་ཆེན། དེ་ལ་བཀྲ་ཤིས་འང་བརྗོད།། --4

སྟོན་ཆེ་བསྐལ་པ་བཟང་པོ་ལ། ཁྲི་ཞིག་བཞེངས་སོང་།

ཅི་དང་ཅི་ཡི། ཁྲི་དེ་བཞེངས་སོང་།

སྨུག་པོ་དུང་གྱི་ཁྲི་ཞིག་བཞེངས་སོང་།

དེ་རྟ་ཤུ་དང་ཤུ་མི་བཞུགས།
དེ་རྟ་ཡབ་ཡུམ་ཕ་མ་བཞུགས་སོང་།
བུ་ནོར་འཛོམ་པོ་ཕ་མ། དེ་ལ་བཀྲ་ཤིས་འང་བརྗོད།། --5

༄༅།།ཀ།། ལྷ་པ་ནི་ན་བཟའ་སྤྱལ་ཅེ།།

༄། མཐོ་བ་རི་གསུམ་རྩེ་ན་བཞུགས་པ། བྱ་རྒོད་པོ་སྤྱན་གསུམ་དེ་བཞུགས།
བསྣམ་མེ་བསྣམ་ལ་ཅི་བརྣམ། བསྣམ་མེ་བསྣམ་ལ་བྱ་སྤྲུ་སྣ་ཚོགས་བསྣམ།
འདོན་ནེ་འདོན་ལ་ཅི་འདོན། འདོན་ནེ་འདོན་ལ་རྒྱུ་སྐར་སྐར་ཚུང་འདོན།
སྐྱེམ་མེ་སྐྱེམ་ལ་ཅི་སྐྱེམ། སྐྱེམ་མེ་སྐྱེམ་ལ་སེང་འབྲུག་རང་ཆང་བསྐྱེམས།།
ཧ་ལི་ལ་ལང་ལ་ལ། ལ་ཧ་ལི་བཀྲ་ཤིས་བརྗོད།། --1

ཤག་མ་དམར་གྱི་འདབས་སུ་བཞུགས་པའི། ཤ་བ་སྤྱན་གསུམ་དེ།།
བསྣམ་མེ་བསྣམ་ལ་ཅི་བསྣམ། བསྣམ་མེ་བསྣམ་ལ་སྤྲིན་ཐུང་ལང་ལིང་བསྣམ།།
འདོན་ནེ་འདོན་ལ་ཅི་འདོན། འདོན་ནེ་འདོན་ལ་མེ་ཏོག་སྣ་ཚོགས་འདོན།།
བསྐྱེམ་མེ་བསྐྱེམ་ལ་ཅི་བསྐྱེམ། བསྐྱེམ་མེ་བསྐྱེམ་ལ་གངས་ཆུ་ཁྲོལ་ཁྲོལ་བསྐྱེམ།།
ཧ་ལི་ལ་ལང་ལ་ལ། ལོ་ཧ་ལི་བཀྲ་ཤིས་བརྗོད།། --2

བྲག་དམར་འདབས་སུ་བཞུགས་པའི། བཙུན་པ་སྤྱན་གསུམ་དེ།
བསྣམ་མེ་བསྣམ་ལ་ཅི་བསྣམ། བསྣམ་མེ་བསྣམ་ལ་རས་གཟན་རྐྱང་གཅིག་བསྣམ།།
འདོན་ནེ་འདོན་ལ་ཅི་འདོན། འདོན་ནེ་འདོན་ལ་འབྲས་དཀར་སྒྲོ་ལོ་འདོན།།
བསྐྱེམ་མེ་བསྐྱེམ་ལ་ཅི་བསྐྱེམ། བསྐྱེམ་མེ་བསྐྱེམ་ལ་སེང་ཆང་སེང་མ་བསྐྱེམ།
ཧ་ལི་ལ་ལང་ལ་ལ། ལ་ཧ་ལི་བཀྲ་ཤིས་བརྗོད།། --3

དཔལ་ལྡན་རྗེ་དུ་བསྒྲུབ་པའི། རྒྱལ་དུ་སྒྲུབ་བསྒྲུབ་ནི།

བསྒྲུབ་ནི་བསྒྲུབ་པ་རྟེ་བསྒྲུབ། བསྒྲུབ་ནི་བསྒྲུབ་པ་པ་ད་མེད་ཤོལ་མེད་བསྒྲུབ།

མཆོད་ནི་མཆོད་པ་རྟེ་མཆོད། མཆོད་ནི་མཆོད་པ་ཆེ་ཟ་ལ་མང་བརྟུད་མཆོད།

བསྐྱེད་ནི་བསྐྱེད་པ་རྟེ་བསྐྱེད། བསྐྱེད་ནི་བསྐྱེད་པ་ཆ་ལ་བརྟུད་རྟེ་བསྐྱེད།

ངེ་པ་བང་པ་ལ། ང་དེ་ཀུ་ཤིས་བཞོག ༤

ཨཱཿཕྱི་པ་རྒྱུ་རྫོང་སྐྱེལ་ཅེ།

སྤྲོ་པོ་བཞིན་རྫོང་བསྐྱོད་པ་ནི། ཤུ་དང་ཤུ་ཡི་དྲིན།

སྐྱང་མ་འཚར་གྱི་དྲིན། དེའི་དྲིན་ལན་བཀས་རྒྱུ་བཞོག།

བདེ་བ་བཟང་བ་ལ། བདེ་བ་ཀྱི་ཤིས་བཞོག། ༡

ཞོ་བྱུ་རྫོང་བསྐྱོད་པ་ནི། ཤུ་དང་ཤུ་ཡི་དྲིན།

ཀླ་མ་འཚར་གྱི་དྲིན། དེའི་དྲིན་ལན་དང་རྒྱུ་བཞོག།

དགེ་བ་བཟང་བ་ལ། བདེ་བ་ཀྱི་ཤིས་བཞོག། ༢

སྐྱང་མ་བཏང་རྫོང་བསྐྱོད་པ་ནི། ཤུ་དང་ཤུ་ཡི་དྲིན།

རྒྱུ་མིག་འཚར་གྱི་དྲིན། དེའི་དྲིན་ལན་དང་རྒྱུ་བཞོག།

དགེ་བ་བཟང་བ་ལ། བདེ་བ་ཀྱི་ཤིས་བཞོག། ༣

ཚ་བྱུ་དང་རྫོང་བསྐྱོད་པ་ནི། ཤུ་དང་ཤུ་ཡི་དྲིན།

བཙུན་ཟམ་སྟོན་མིའི་དྲིན། དེའི་དྲིན་ལན་དང་རྒྱུ་བཞོག།

དགེ་བ་བཟང་བ་ལ། བདེ་བ་ཀྱི་ཤིས་བཞོག། ༤

རྫོང་བསྐྱམས་པ་དེ། སུ་དང་སུ་ཡི་དྲིན།
ཡབ་དང་ཡུམ་གྱི་དྲིན། དེའི་དྲིན་ལན་དཀར་ཆུ་བརྗོད།
ཏ་ལི་ལ་ལང་ལ་ལ། ལ་ཏ་ལི་བཀྲ་ཤིས་བརྗོད།། --5

༄༅།།༧།། བདུན་པ་མེན་ཏོག་འབུལ་ཆེ།།

རྒྱ་གར་གྱི་རྒྱལ་པོ། བདེ་ཝོ་སྐྱུ་ཁམས་བཟང་།
རྒྱལ་མོའིས་ཚིག་ལེགས་གསུངས། མེན་ཏོག་ཙམ་ཟམ་འཁྲུངས།
ཤིས་ཏ་ལོ་ཙམ་ཟམ་འཁྲུངས།། --1

མེན་ཏོག་བཀྲུད་ཟམ་འཁྲུངས། ཤིས་ཏ་ལོ་བཀྲུད་ཟམ་འཁྲུངས།
གཅིག་ནི་ཡང་མེན་ཏོག། གཅིག་ནི་ཏ་ལོ།
བདེ་ཝོ་སུ་ལ་འབུལ། ཤིས་ཏ་ལོ་སུ་ལ་འབུལ།
སྟེང་ཕྱོགས་ལྷ་ལ་འབུལ། ཤིས་ལྷ་ལ་འབུལ་བའི།
བདེ་ཝོ་བཀྲ་ཤིས་བརྗོད།། --2

གཉིས་ནི་ཡང་མེན་ཏོག། གཉིས་ནི་ཏ་ལོ།
བདེ་ཝོ་སུ་ལ་འབུལ། ཤིས་ཏ་ལོ་སུ་ལ་འབུལ།
བར་ཕྱོགས་བཙན་ལ་འབུལ། ཤིས་བཙན་ལ་འབུལ་བའི།
བདེ་ཝོ་བཀྲ་ཤིས་བརྗོད།། --3

གསུམ་ནི་ཡང་མེ་ཏོག། གསུམ་ནི་ཏ་ལོ།
བདེ་ཝོ་སུ་ལ་འབུལ། ཤིས་ཏ་ལོ་སུ་ལ་འབུལ།
འོག་ཕྱོགས་ཀླུ་ལ་འབུལ། ཤིས་ཀླུ་ལ་འབུལ་བའི།
བདེ་ཝོ་བཀྲ་ཤིས་བརྗོད།། --4

བཞི་ནི་ཡང་མེན་ཏོག།། བཞི་ནི་ཏ་ལོ།
བདེ་བོ་སུ་ལ་འབུལ། ཤེས་ཏ་ལོ་སུ་ལ་འབུལ།
ཨ་བ་ཡབ་ལ་འབུལ། ཤེས་ཡབ་ལ་འབུལ་བའི།
བདེ་བོ་བཀྲ་ཤིས་བརྗོད། --5

ལྔ་ནི་ཡང་མེན་ཏོག། ལྔ་ནི་ཏ་ལོ།
བདེ་བོ་སུ་ལ་འབུལ། ཤེས་ཏ་ལོ་སུ་ལ་འབུལ།
ཨ་མ་ཡུམ་ལ་འབུལ། ཤེས་ཡུམ་ལ་འབུལ་བའི།
བདེ་བོ་བཀྲ་ཤིས་བརྗོད།།--6

དྲུག་ནི་ཡང་མེན་ཏོག། དྲུག་ནི་ཏ་ལོ།
བདེ་བོ་སུ་ལ་འབུལ། ཤེས་ཏ་ལོ་སུ་ལ་འབུལ།
ཨ་ཙོ་སྲས་ལ་འབུལ། ཤེས་ཨ་ཙོ་སྲས་ལ་འབུལ་བའི།
བདེ་བོ་བཀྲ་ཤིས་བརྗོད། --7

བདུན་ནི་ཡང་མེ་ཏོག་ བདུན་ནི་ཏ་ལོ།
བདེ་བོ་སུ་ལ་འབུལ། ཤེས་ཏ་ལོ་སུ་ལ་འབུལ།
ཨ་ཅེ་ལྕམ་ལ་འབུལ། ཤེས་ཨ་ཅེ་ལྕམ་ལ་འབུལ་བའི།
བདེ་བོ་བཀྲ་ཤིས་བརྗོད།། --8

བརྒྱད་ནི་ཡང་མེན་ཏོག། བརྒྱད་ནི་ཏ་ལོ།
བདེ་བོ་སུ་ལ་འབུལ། ཤེས་ཏ་ལོ་སུ་ལ་འབུལ།
ཨ་བོ་རང་ལ་འབུལ། ཤེས་ཨ་བོ་རང་ལ་འབུལ་བའི།
བདེ་བོ་བཀྲ་ཤིས་བརྗོད།། --9

Note: Manuscripts consulted:

1. Tashi Lha-rgyal of Khangsar.
2. Tashi Karingpa, of Karing.
3. Amchi Gyaltshan, Tino.
4. Old Song Lyrics in Bhoti Culture, Lahaul from Dartse.
5. sTod Ghati Kalyan Sabha, Kyelang.
6. (Roerich, 1934: 126-147).

Reference

Roerich, George De. 1934. The Tibetan Dialects of Lahul (83-189), Tibetica I, Journal of Urusvati Himalayan Research Institute, Vol. III, of the Roerich Museum, Naggar (Kullu) and New York.

4

Lha-rgyas : Prayer to the God

Tobdan

The following song, entitled Lhargyas (lha-rgyas) which may be translated, not properly, as 'Prayer to god', is an ancient ceremonial song which is still in practice in sTod. Its original is lost but many people have kept it in writing for the purpose of singing. But it is difficult to extract the meaning fully. An attempt has been made to restore and make the prayer-song clearer and meaningful. No attempt has been made to put the composition in verse form. Its flow has been maintained as it is sung. The song has several names. It is purely of folk tradition. It belongs to the period before the advent of Tibetan Buddhism in the area. The song has some indication of its contact with the Indian Buddhism. It is sung specially at the time of Losar, the New Year festival.

Translation

I. In the beginning Auspiciousness

In the beginning may there come auspiciousness!
He has come there in the firmament.
May he come. May he come in the firmament.
May auspiciousness come in the firmament.
May the man come in. May the man come.
There is throne for sitting in the middle.
May he come in the middle of firmament above.
May he come. May he come.

He has reached at the place of sitting in the middle of firmament above,

May he come. Pronounce auspiciousness! ..1

In the beginning may there come auspiciousness!

He has come there over the glacier.

May he come. May he come over the glacier.

May auspiciousness come over the glacier.

May the man come in. May the man come.

This is the place of sitting for the Great Lion.

May he come in the middle over the glacier above.

May he come.

He has reached at the place of sitting in the middle over the glacier above.

May he come, Say auspiciousness! 2

In the beginning may there come auspiciousness!

He has come there in the forest.

May auspiciousness come in the forest.

May the man come in. May the man come.

This is the place of sitting for the Great Tiger.

May he come in the middle of forest above.

May he come.

He has reached at the place of sitting in the middle of forest above.

May he come. Say auspiciousness!. ..3

In the beginning may there come auspiciousness!

He has come there in the lake.

May he come. May he come in the lake.

May auspiciousness come to the lake.

May the man come in. May the man come.

This is the place of sitting for the Great Fish.

May he come in the middle of the lake above.

May he come.

He has reached at the place of sitting in the middle of the Lake above.

May he come, Pronounce auspiciousness!. ..4

In the beginning may there come auspiciousness!

He has come in the castle.

May he come. May he come in the castle.

May auspicious come in the castle.

May he come in, May the man come.

This is the place of sitting for the Great Man.

May he come in the middle in the castle above.

May he come.

He has reached at the place of sitting in the middle of the castle above.

May he come. Pronounce auspiciousness!. .5

In the beginning may there come auspiciousness!

He has come there at the ground of prosperity.

May he come. May he come at the ground of prosperity.

May the man come in. May the man come.

This is the place of sitting for the honourable Father and Mother.

May he come.

He has reached at the place of sitting in the middle of the prosperous house above.

May he come. Pronounce auspiciousness!. ..6

II. Song of Gathering

Sitting in the firmament above, the Sun, on the throne with parasol, looks admirable.

Sitting in the firmament below, the white shining Moon, looks admirable.

Assembled in the middle of firmament above, the stars who

are happy to assemble, look admirable. Then one, two, three... There is need of a companion for assembling. Pronounce Auspiciousness! ..1

Sitting on the glacier above, the white Great Lion looks admirable.

While sitting over the glacier below, his beautiful manes look admirable.

Assembled in the middle over the glacier above, the lion cubs who are happy to assemble, look admirable.

Then one two three....

There is need of a companion for assembling. Pronounce Auspiciousness! 2

Sitting in the forest above, the Great Tiger with variegated colours, looks admirable. While sitting in the forest below, the beautiful lines look admirable.

Assembled in the middle of the forest above, the little tiger cubs who are happy to assemble, look admirable.

Then one two three... There is need of a companion for assembling. Pronounce Auspiciousness! 3

Sitting in the lake above, the Great Fish, always wavering, looks admirable. While sitting in the lake below, his beautiful golden eyes look admirable. Assembled in the middle of the lake above, the little fishes who are happy to assemble, look admirable. Then one, two, Three,... There is need of a companion for assembling. Pronounce Auspiciousness! 4.

Sitting in the castle above, the Great Man, uppermost in the row, looks admirable. While sitting in the castle below, his high lineage looks admirable.

Assembled in the middle of the castle, the householders who are happy to assemble, look admirable. Then one, two, three... There is need of a companion for assembling. Pronounce Auspiciousness! 5.

Sitting on the ground above, the honourable Father and Mother look admirable. Sitting on the ground below, the richness of wealth of offsprings looks admirable. Then one, two, three... There is need of a companion for assembling. Pronounce Auspiciousness!..6

III. Pitching the Tent

In the middle of the firmament above, a tent was pitched. Of what material it is made of, the tent that was pitched. Is of yellow silk, the tent that was pitched.

Of yellow colour, of gold, is the tent that was pitched.

Who were those pitching the tent-poles? 1

The Sun sitting over the throne with parasol pitched the tent-poles. Who were those tying the tent with stitching-ropes. The multitude of stars stitched the stitching-ropes. Pronounce auspiciousness for stitching the tent with stitching-ropes.

In the middle of the glacier above, a tent was pitched. Of what material it is made of, the tent that was pitched. Is of white silk, the tent was pitched.

Who were those pitching the tent-poles. The white Great Lion pitched the tent-poles. Who were those stitching the tent with stitching-ropes? There were many lion cubs who stitched the tent with stitching-ropes. Pronounce auspiciousness for stitching the tent with stitching-ropes. 2

In the middle of the forest above, a tent was pitched. Of what material is it made of, the tent that was pitched.

Is of silk of particolour, the tent that was pitched.

Who were those pitching the tent-poles? The Great Tiger of variegated colours pitched the tent. Who were those stitching the tent with stitching-ropes. There were many tiger cubs who stitched the tent with stitching-ropes. Pronounce auspicious for stitching the tent with stitching-ropes. 3

In the middle of the lake above, a tent was pitched. Of what material is it made of, the tent that was pitched. Is of green silk, the tent that was pitched.

Who were those pitching the tent-poles? The Great Fish who moves in wavering manner pitched the tent-poles. Who were those stitching the tent with stitching-ropes? There were many little fishes stitching the tent with stitching-ropes. Pronounce auspiciousness for stitching the tent with stitching-ropes. 4

In the middle of castle above, a tent was pitched. Of what material was it made of, the tent that was pitched. Is of grey silk, the tent that was pitched.

Who pitched the tent-poles? The Great Man, uppermost in the row pitched the tent -poles. Who were those stitching the tent with stitching-ropes There were many householders who stitched the tent with the stitching-ropes. Pronounce auspiciousness for stitching the tent with the stitching-ropes. 5

On the ground in the middle above, a tent was pitched. Of what material was it made of, the tent that was pitched. Is of blue silk, the tent that was pitched.

Who were those pitching the tent-poles? The honourable Father and Mother pitched the tent-poles. Who were those stitching the tent with stitching-ropes. There were many relatives who stitched the tent with stitching-ropes. Pronounce auspiciousness for stitching the tent with stitching-ropes...6

IV. Raising Throne

In the former times, in the *bhadra-kalpa,* the blessed kalpa, a throne was raised. Of what material, the throne that was raised, is made of? Of yellow colour, made of Gold, the throne was raised. Who are the persons who sit on the throne? Thereon sits the god of the above.

For the god whose head is held high, pronounce auspiciousness.. ..1

In the former times, in the *bhadra-kalpa*, the blessed kalpa, a throne was raised. Of what material, the throne that was raised, is made of? Of white colour. made of silver, the throne was raised. Who are the persons who sit on the throne? Thereon sits bTsan (the god named) of the middle region (the region between the earth and the sky). For bTsan of the good 'Gangs-ri' (Kailash mountain), pronounce auspiciousness. …2

In the former times, in the *bhadra-kalpa,* the blessed kalpa, a throne was raised. Of what material, the throne that was raised, is made of? Of green colour, made of turquoise, the throne was raised. Who are the persons who sit on the throne? There sits the Naga, the Serpent god, of the nether world. For the friendly Naga of the blue and deep Turquise Lake (Mansarovar), Pronounce auspiciousness,.3

In the former times, in the *bhadra-kalpa,* the blessed kalpa, a throne was raised. Of what material, the throne that was raised, is made of? Of grey colour, made of crystal, the throne was raised. Who are the persons who sit on the throne? There sits the Great Man, the uppermost in the row. For the Great Man of the high lineage, pronounce auspiciousness. …4

In the former times, in the *bhadra-kalpa,* the blessed kalpa, a throne was raised. Of what material, the throne that has been raised, is made of? Of purple colour, made of Conch-shell, the throne was raised. Who are the persons who sit on the throne? There sit the honourable Father and Mother. For the honourable Father and Mother, blessed with the wealth of offsprings, pronounce auspiciousness….5

V. Offering Garments

Sitting on the peaks of three high mountains, there are three wild eagle brothers.

They wear, but what do they wear? They wear various kinds of feathers.

They eat, but what do they eat? For meal, they eat small stars. They drink, but what do they drink? For drinking, they drink the very beer of Dragon and White Lion. Pronounce auspiciousness. …1

Sitting beside the red gravels, there are three stag brothers. They wear, but what do they wear? They wear the small slices of light cloud. They eat, but what do they eat? They eat numerous kinds of flowers. They drink, but what do they drink? They drink the gurgling water of the glacier. Pronounce auspiciousness…..2

Sitting beside the red rock, there are three monk brothers. They wear, but what do they wear? They wear robes of a single length of cloth. They eat, but what do they eat? They eat white rice grains each separated. They drink, but what do they drink? They drink pure kind of beer. Pronounce auspiciousness. …3

Sitting in the prosperous house above, there are three prince brothers. They wear, but what do they wear? They wear costly silken clothes. They eat, but what do they eat? They eat delicious healthy food. They drink, but what do they drink. They drink *arag* (wine) that is like ambrosia. Pronounce auspiciousness. …4

VI. Offering of Crown

'Srolo' (a grass), wearing golden crown (flower), due to whose kindness is this. This is due to the kindness of the red grassy land. The cause of its kindness is the water from the glacier. Pronounce auspiciousness….1

'Nyalo', wearing a turban, due to whose kindness is this? This is due to the kindness of the red gravels. The cause of the kindness is the water from the frozen ice. Pronounce auspiciousness…..2

'gLang-ma', wearing woolly turban, due to whose kindness is this? This is due to the kindness of the red water spring (water spring at the red earth). The cause of the kindness is the water from the frozen ice. Pronounce auspiciousness. …3

'Om-boog', wearing silky crown, due to whose kindness is this. This is due to the kindness of blue water of the river. The cause of the kindness is the water from the frozen ice. Pronounce auspiciousness. …4

The Prince wearing turban, due to whose kindness is this? This is due to the kindness of the honourable Father and Mother. The cause of this kindness is the white water. Pronounce auspiciousness. …5

VII. Offering of Flowers

King of India, may he be happy and healthy. Oh, words of the Queen are pleasing. Tell, how many flowers have grown? How many auspicious flowers of *ha-lo* (a wild flower) have grown? About eight flowers have grown. About eight auspicious flowers of *ha-lo* have grown. –1.

Firstly the flower, firstly the auspicious flower of *ha-lo*, to whom should it be offered? Firstly the flower, the auspicious flower of *ha-lo*, offer it to the god above. For auspiciously offering the auspicious flower to the god above, pronounce auspiciousness. —2.

Secondly offer the auspicious flower to ….bTsan, the god of the middle region ….3

Thirdly offer the auspicious flower to …. The Naga god, (of Nether region)….4

Fourthly offer the auspicious flower to … Father….5

Fifthly offer the auspicious flower to …. Mother ….6

Sixthly offer the auspicious flower to …. Brother … 7

Seventhly offer the auspicious flower to ….. Sister….8

Eighthly offer the auspicious flower to .. us, ourselves (you and we)…9

• • •

1. View of Tinno Village

2. Lha-shug, Sacred Juniper Tree Dedicated to Village Deity

3. Ruined Pala Gonpa

4. View of the Zong Gonpa

5. Zong Gonpa and Chorten

6. Carved Wooden Bracket and Door Frames

7. Wooden Altar

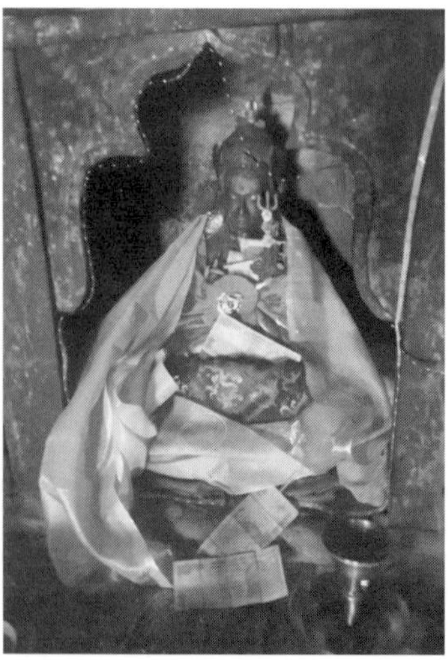

8. Padmasambhava

9. Elevan Headed Avalokiteswara

10. Avalokiteswara and Padmasambhava

11. Bronze Lokeswara

12. Lama Gyaltshan Bokarpa

13. Lama Rigzin

14. Lama Nawang Rigzin

15. Local Ladies waiting for the Chief Guest

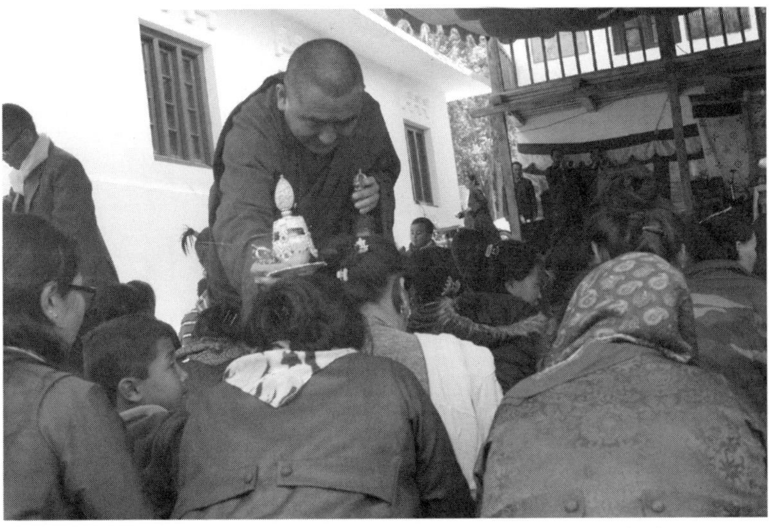

16. Chhogon Rinpochhe (Tanzin Chhoeki Gyatsho)

17. Lamas during Religious Discourse

18. Lama Gyapho in the discourse

19. Lama Chhering Wangyal (left) and Chhewang Namgyal (right)

20. Lama Dondub Thinley

21. Local Residents of the Village during Religious Ceremonies

22. Local Residents of the Village during Religious Ceremonies